CHRISTOPHER COLUMBUS

The Discovery of the New World

Written by Romain Parmentier
In collaboration with Fabrizio Melai
Translated by Rose Brichard

History 

CHRISTOPHER COLUMBUS

KEY INFORMATION

- **Born:** Between 25 August and 31 October 1451 in Genoa (Republic of Genoa)
- **Died:** The 20 May 1506 in Valladolid (Republic of Spain)
- **Goal of expeditions:** Mark out a commercial route to Asia and the East Indies travelling westward
- **Explored regions of the world:**
  - First voyage: The Bahamas, Cuba, Hispaniola (Haiti)
  - Second voyage: The Lesser Antilles, Jamaica
  - Third voyage: Trinidad, South America, the mouth of the Orinoco River (South American river)
  - Fourth voyage: The Honduran, Costa Rican and Panamanian coasts (Central America)
- **Most notable discovery:** The American continent

INTRODUCTION

"As the Pinta was the finest ship and went before the admiral nave, it was she who discovered the land" (Balard, 1992)[1]

At 2am on 12 October 1492, 33 days since Christopher Columbus and the crews of his three ships departed from the edge of the world's mapped territory. They had set off into a new world hoping to reach Asia, unaware of the discovery they were about to make.

---

1. All quotes from this text have been translated by 50Minutes.com

It was not, however, such an easy goal to reach. For years the explorer's project had been judged unachievable and refused support and funding. His objective was indeed major: to find a new westward route to the East Indies, seen as symbols of wealth and prosperity due to the spices and gold to be found there. It was not until April 1492 that Columbus' expedition was finally approved by the Spanish crown. His epic saga was just beginning.

Christopher Columbus embarked on four westward voyages towards what we now know is the American continent, though at the time he was unaware of this. Each of these journeys featured significant discoveries and contributed to the development of the geography and our understanding of the world. However, exploring new lands would also go hand in hand with colonisation, something which would profoundly shape Spanish history. Spain became one of the most powerful countries of the modern era; as Europe emerged from the middle ages, it readied itself for world domination.

Portrait of Christopher Columbus painted around 1835 by Antoine Maurin

CHILDHOOD AND EDUCATION

Christopher Columbus was a navigator and explorer. He was the first European of the modern era to cross the Atlantic and reach the American continent, which was at the time undiscovered and uncharted territory. He was born some point between 25 August and 31 October 1451 in Genoa to an ordinary family; the destiny which awaited him was far-removed from his humble beginnings. The oldest child of a modest weaver, his most important duty was to learn his father's trade. The young Columbus was not at all inspired by this prospect and eventually renounced this line of work altogether. He then became a sailor and embarked on several commercial voyages in the Mediterranean, meanwhile acquiring a strong awareness of the world's mapped territory through his own personal research and studies.

THE LONG-AWAITED VENTURE

In 1476, Columbus set off for Portugal, a country in which seafaring exploration was already established. It was here that the navigator refined his plan to reach the East via the Atlantic, while the rest of the world had its sights set on circumnavigating Africa to reach the same destination. Between 1484 and 1485, Columbus decided to share his proposal with John II (1455-1495), King of Portugal. When the latter refused to finance an expedition so seemingly unachievable, Columbus left Lisbon for Spain, humiliated and crippled by debt. In January 1486, the Catholic monarchs Isabella of Castile (1451-1504) and Ferdinand II of Aragon (1452-1516) received him at court. Despite their interest in his proposition, their resources were tied up in the effort to reconquer Granada, which was at the time ruled by the Moors (Andalusian Muslims). Columbus' quest was therefore held in suspense.

However, his hopes were reignited by the defeat and annexation of Granada in 1492; his time had finally come. He met once again with the Spanish Crown who in turn approved his plans. The contract was formalised in April 1492 in the "Capitulations of Santa Fe". Columbus was given the title of Admiral of the Ocean Sea by the King and Queen, in addition to the rank of viceroy and the right to govern any territory which he should discover. The Genoese sailor could finally begin the quest of a lifetime.

THE EXPEDITIONS

The epic voyage began on 3 August 1492. They departed from Palos, a promontory on the Spanish coast. Passing through the Canary Islands, Columbus set off towards the west. This was the start of a long journey. It was not until late at night on 11 October that land came into view once again; Columbus believed himself to have reached Asia. In fact, he had just encountered the Bahamas, Cuba and Hispaniola. On returning to Spain in 1493, he immediately set about preparing a second voyage, this time with the aim of colonising the land. Once he had established a colony on Hispaniola, he continued his exploration and discovered the various Caribbean islands before returning to Europe in 1496. Two years later, he was once again at sea on his third voyage. He cast anchor on the South American continent for the first time and discovered Trinidad. He then returned to the Spanish colony on Hispaniola but was unable to defeat a rebellion led against him and found himself stripped of his title and arrested by the settlers. He was sent back to Spain in 1500 where he was imprisoned for his failed colonial governance and the slave trade which he had developed. He was freed by the Spanish sovereigns and departed once again in 1502, this time searching for a passage towards the East Indies. Instead, he struck the Central American coasts.

Subjected to a violent storm, the voyage took a disastrous turn and Columbus was forced to return to Spain in 1504 for the last time. He died on 20 May 1506 in Valladolid, convinced of having discovered a Western route to Asia, not a new continent.

POLITICAL, SOCIAL AND ECONOMIC CONTEXT

THE DAWN OF THE AGE OF DISCOVERY

While Christopher Columbus is at the heart of one of the greatest discoveries of modern history, he was not the first to set sail with the hope of finding new lands and new trade routes. Even in the 13th century, Europeans followed the example of Marco Polo the Venetian traveller (1254-1324) in setting out on the Silk Road in order to discover Asia and its marvels. However, the Age of Discovery did not begin in earnest until the 15th century, particularly with regards to the Atlantic coasts. At the heart of this leap forwards which would open Europe up to the world was a young Portuguese prince: Henri, nicknamed Henry the Navigator (1394-1460), the third son of King John I (1357-1433).

Having driven out the Moors, the newly independent Portugal found its new vocation in the world of maritime exploration thanks to the young Prince Henri. Fascinated by geography and the ancient texts which Europe was beginning to rediscover, the Prince intended to put his name in the history books. He therefore launched a campaign of maritime development in Portugal, meanwhile surrounding himself by intellectuals and founding a school of navigation in Sagres (Cape St. Vincent), where he promoted technological advancement.

Over the course of the 15th century, the number of expeditions multiplied. The explorers and those funding them were motivated by hopes of finding gold, opening agricultural markets, discovering new routes leading to the East Indies, but also by the legend of the kingdom of Prester John. In 1418, the Portuguese discovered Madeira, followed by the Azores in 1427. Among many other explorations, they then went on to trace Cape Bojador (Western Sahara) in 1434, Cape Verde in 1445 and discovered the mouth of the Senegal River. They claimed the coasts of Africa, moving beyond the Cape of Good Hope in 1488. These new initiatives clearly fascinated people at the time and the taste for adventure gradually permeated across Europe.

GOOD TO KNOW

The Kingdom of Prester John is a mysterious mythical Christian kingdom. According to legend, it is situated somewhere in the East. The origins of the myth can be traced to the Middle Ages, with the kingdom's location changing from Central Asia to China to India and East Africa according to different accounts. The importance of this legend should be underlined; Europeans confronted by Islamic expansion imagined Prester John as a major ally who would allow them to encircle and triumph over the Arabs and the Turks. As such, the quest for the Kingdom of Prester John motivated maritime exploration and plays a key role in the beginning of the Age of Discovery.

THE FALL OF CONSTANTINOPLE AND ITS CONSEQUENCES

The exploration of new maritime routes began in the 15th century, but a key event accelerated the expedition movement. On 29 May 1453, the Ottoman Sultan Mehmed II (1432-1481) ended nearly one thousand years of the Byzantine tradition when he seized Constantinople, the capital of the Byzantine Empire. Considered by Europeans as the gateway to the East, the city was from that point onwards annexed by the Ottoman Empire; this was to have a direct impact on maritime exploration.

Harbouring numerous intellectual centres within, the Byzantine Empire had kept knowledge within its borders during the entire course of its history. This included geographical knowledge inherited from ancient times and from the Arab and Byzantine traditions. However, the fall of the empire led to an exodus of intellectuals and thinkers towards Western Europe, who brought with them their skills and knowledge and part of their incredible heritage with them. Amid these changes and new arrivals, Europeans rediscovered texts from antiquity and of the Arab world. Ancient models of the world, such as that presented by Ptolemy (Greek writer, astronomer, geographer and mathematician, roughly 100-170 AD) therefore reappeared and further cultivated the spirit of adventure of the time. Despite the measurement errors in the Ptolemaic model, the rediscovery of these works reanimated ideas concerning the earth's spherical form and means of identifying locations through geographic coordinates.

The fall of Constantinople also had an immediate impact on East-West trade relations; Eastern merchants selling highly-sought after goods such as silk, spices and incense often passed through the city. However, Constantinople's fall and the Ottoman expansion which followed equally led to higher taxes which therefore slowed commercial growth. As such, the search for new trade routes became of major importance for Europeans, who dreamed of reaching the East Indies while avoiding the Ottoman middle-man.

THE END OF THE RECONQUISTA AND THE EMERGENCE OF EUROPE

The year 1492 was a momentous one, not only for Christopher Columbus but for Spain: the country put an end to eight centuries of Moorish occupation in certain parts of the its territory. After reconquering Granada on 2 January 1492, the Catholic monarchs Isabella of Castile and Ferdinand II of Aragon were able to unite Spain and thus end the Reconquista. The country was therefore able to consider maritime exploration and compete with neighbouring Portugal. The Spanish Crown also had a religious motivation for exploration; they intended to spread Christianity and evangelise new lands.

The Surrender of Granada, painting by Francisco Pradilla and Ortiz, 1882

The whole of Europe was in a state of flux. There was marked progress in numerous domains which drove the continent to expand its outlook and vision beyond its own borders. Plague epidemics became rarer and the population gradually grew. The revival of cities gave rise to the emergence of an entrepreneurial bourgeoisie hungry for profit. Over time, feudal systems faded away, replaced by states with a desire to extend their property.

However, Europe was facing new challenges. From the East, the Arabs and Turks; numerous crusades proved incapable of diminishing this threat. Not only were spice trade routes blocked, so too was the European capacity to procure gold, and therefore make money, in sub-Saharan Africa. Europe's finances were therefore significantly constrained, leading to serious economic crises between 1330 and 1450. The search for precious materials to supply the various European states gained new importance in the wake of these financial difficulties.

Lastly, the advances made in geography and cartography must be taken into account. In 1492, German cosmographer and navigator Martin Behaim (1459-1507) designed the world's first terrestrial globe. From then on, a cartography designed only for navigators appeared on the scene. Portolan navigational charts and their systems of wind roses and scales made maritime expeditions more precise.

THE GENESIS OF A GREAT ADVENTURE

A tireless reader of antique texts, the voyages of Marco Polo and the *Imago Mundi* by French prelate and theologian Pierre d'Ailly (1350-1420), Columbus was intent on making himself a success. He knew that the earth was round and his own reading had made him certain of one thing: the Atlantic Ocean was not as wide as it seemed. From this perspective, the westward journey from Europe to the Orient seemed feasible and presented an irresistible opportunity to escape the constraints imposed by the Arab markets or the long journey around the African coasts.

Columbus made calculations based on those of Marinus of Tyre (Greek geographer, 1st – 2nd century AD) and Ptolemaic theory; they were far-removed from geographic reality. He was initially convinced that Europe, Africa and Asia covered 62.5% of the globe; in fact, they represent only 36.11%, meaning that the world's mapped territories were proportionally smaller and the seas larger. He estimated the earth's circumference at 30 000 kilometres, 10 000 kilometres less than the true figure. From these mistaken calculations, Columbus estimated the distance between the Canary Islands and the rich Cipangu Island (medieval Japanese name) at 4 400 kilometres instead of the true 22 000 kilometres.

In any case, if he had known the real distance, perhaps he would never have attempted such a voyage. So when Columbus caught sight of land on 12 October 1492, it was where he expected to find it; the idea that he had discovered a whole new continent would not have crossed his mind. Instead, he would have felt that he had succeeded in his quest to find Cipangu and Asia.

THE EXPEDITION

Other than his titles and the likely riches to come, the Capitulations of Santa Fe granted Columbus only limited resources. The Spanish Crown loaned him 2 million *maravedís* (bronze currency) to equip three vessels supplied by the town of Palos. In Palos, he met shipowner Martin Alonso Yanez Pinzon (1440-1493) and he provided Columbus with two ships: the *Pinta* (the spotted one) and the *Niña* (the little girl), the ships' names evoking those of prostitutes.

At the time, the caravel ship was the vessel best equipped for navigating the high seas. Though it was first designed in the 13th century, various innovations between then and Columbus' time made it all the more efficient. 15th century caravels were made with less wood, making them lighter and thus limiting the draught (the height of the submerged part of the boat). This improved their performance and manoeuvrability. At around 23 meters in length and 6.5 meters in breadth, the caravel had four masts, each of which was equipped with square sails and one triangular sail for propulsion.

The caravel which would have been used during Christopher Columbus' era

Christopher Columbus was convinced that a third ship was needed, and he eventually took Juan de la Cosa (roughly 1449-1510) up on his offer, buying a carrack (another large vessel-type) called the *Gallega*. This ship, more rounded than the caravel, was more imposing but slower and capable of carrying up to 110 tonnes compared to just 60 in the caravel's case. Columbus immediately renamed her the *Santa Maria*. This would be the flagship which would carry the majority of the provisions.

The Admiral Columbus' next task was to recruit a crew for

each vessel. For many, Columbus' expedition would be a one-way journey; the fear and uncertainty which would have been felt by those thinking of joining up was entirely merited. Despite the fact that theories had proven the world to be round, no-one had actually shown this to be true. To do so would mean conquering the Atlantic Ocean - the dark sea, populated by all kinds of sea monsters according to legend. Nonetheless, Columbus managed to assemble enough sailors seeking their fortune:

- 22 men on board the *Niña*
- 26 men on board the *Pinta*
- 39 men on board the *Santa Maria*

With 15 months' worth of food supplies and six months' worth of water supplies on board, everything was finally ready. Now the adventure could begin.

REACHING THE EAST BY THE WEST

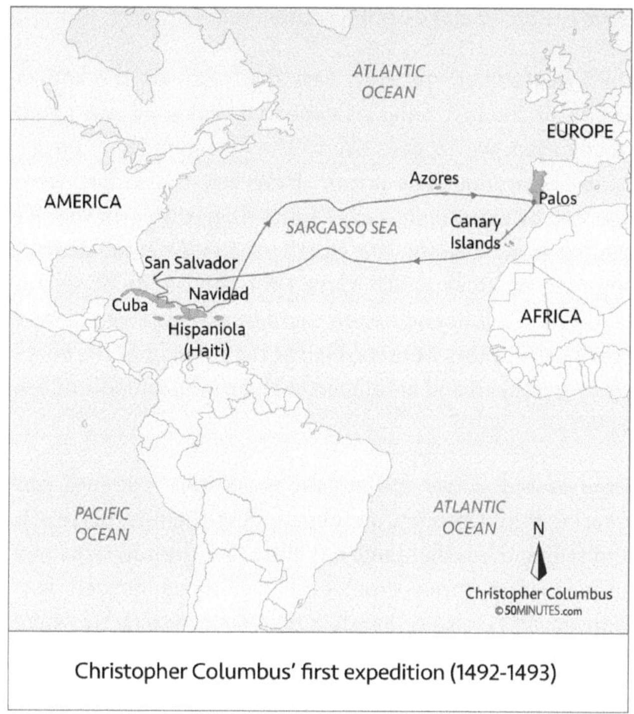

Christopher Columbus' first expedition (1492-1493)

Columbus and his crew departed from Palos on the morning of 3 August 1492. Despite their goal being to travel west, they first headed south towards the Canaries, with trade winds favourable to an ocean passage. After just three days of sailing, trouble had already begun: the *Pinta*'s rudders broke. A makeshift repair meant the *Pinta* arrived in the Canaries just a few days after the Niña and the Santa Maria.

Unable to find another boat, Columbus was forced to wait until the repairs were complete. He and his crew did not leave the archipelago until 6 September.

On 9 September, the crew cast their eyes on the known world for the last time. As expected, the wind was good, strong even, which gave rise to the first glimpse of uncertainty regarding their return. However, the sailors were haunted by other fears. On 17 September, they came across the Sargasso Sea (to the North of the Atlantic Ocean), engulfed by algae which spread for thousands of square feet. While this phenomenon could be read as a sign of land nearby, the sailors were terrified at the thought of the boats getting trapped and entangled in algae in the middle of the ocean.

Time passed slowly and already the sailors' patience was wearing thin. Despite Columbus urging them to persevere and telling them that land was close, the horizon remained empty. After some time, even Columbus himself was worried; on 1 October, he could no longer say exactly where they were. Tension mounted and on 10 October, Columbus narrowly avoided a mutiny in the ranks by proposing a compromise: if they did not see land in three days, he would consider turning back.

On Thursday 11 October, the crew caught sight of pieces of wood floating around the ships in the ocean, one of which was cut with a razor-straight edge; there was no doubt, land was close, and it was inhabited.

At 2am on 12 October, they saw their salvation. "Land ho!"

The cry went up from one of the *Pinta*'s sailors, Rodrigo de Triana (born roughly 1469). Columbus called the first island San Salvador; it was beautiful and indeed inhabited. Though he had just discovered the Bahamas, Columbus thought it was the East Indies, and thus called the island's inhabitants "Indians". They were in awe of the Spaniards, and presented themselves naked, covered only by body paint. When the bargaining began, the Spanish crew soon realised the indigenous people possessed neither gold nor spices.

Painting depicting Christopher Columbus haggling over goods with the Native Americans

On 14 October, Columbus decided to set off once more, and passed from island to island. When he reached Cuba on 28 October, he thought he had found Cipangu. Except for bracelets, belts and rings, gold was nowhere to be found any notable quantity. Unaware that Cuba was in fact an island, Columbus eventually decided that it must be the edge of the Asian continent. On continuing his journey, he saw yet another island, named Cibao by the indigenous population. Once again, he believed that this must be the long-awaited Cipangu island; fact he had just set foot on Haiti. His hopes were quickly extinguished and the island was renamed Hispaniola. As the expedition continued, so did the encounters and negotiations with the indigenous peoples. On Christmas Day, disaster struck: the *Santa Maria* ran aground. The sailors were safe, but there were too many of them for the two other caravels to carry, forcing some of them to stay where they were. In these circumstances, Christopher Columbus founded Navidad, a small fort on the coast of Hispaniola.

After amassing everything he could find to impress the Spanish King and Queen, including several indigenous people, Columbus decided it was time to return. On 16 January 1493, the *Pinta* and the *Niña* set off for Europe in troubled waters - several sailors almost drowned. On 15 February, the Azores came into view once again and one month later, Christopher Columbus was back in Palos. He received a hero's welcome, with everyone convinced that he had in fact fulfilled his quest of reaching Asia by sailing west.

THE FIRST COLONY

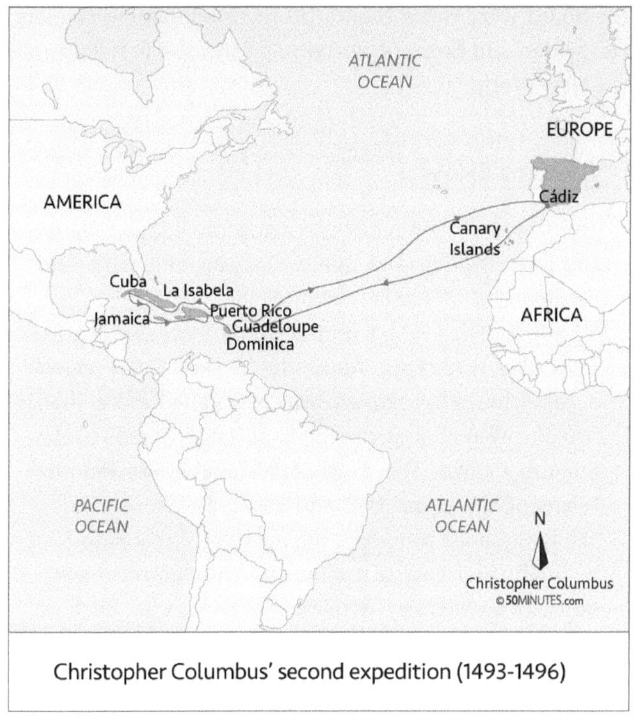

Christopher Columbus' second expedition (1493-1496)

The Catholic monarchs were delighted by Columbus' success and keen to re-establish their lost empire. In June 1494, they achieved their goal when they signed Treaty of Tordesillas. However, the time had now come to go back and provide for those who had stayed, and above all begin to conquer the new lands and make use of their resources. In less than five months, a second expedition was organised and equipped with everything needed. This time not just three but seventeen ships left from Cádiz, Spain on 25 September 1493. On board were more than 1200 men; noblemen, soldiers, clergymen and farmers who would form the first colony in the New World.

Passing once again through the Canaries, Christopher Columbus chose a more south-westerly route on his second voyage which led him to discover the Lesser Antilles - Dominica to be exact - on 3 November 1493. The following day he discovered Guadeloupe, Santa Cruz on the 14th and Puerto Rico on the 19th. The sailors' moral was high, but on returning to Hispaniola and Navidad on 27 November, there was a palpable sense of disillusionment. The men they had left there were dead; some of them had killed one another, others were unable to survive sickness and others still had suffered at the hands of the Native population who sought revenge for their own exploitation. Setting off towards the East, Christopher Columbus found a site for his first colony and named it Isabella after the queen. On 6 January 1994, mass was held there for the first time.

In April 1494, Columbus sailed around the edge of Southern Cuba, trying to establish whether or not this land was an island. The admiral turned back too soon and officially declared that Cuba was the edge of Asia. On 5 May, he reached Jamaica, bringing the number of newly-discovered islands to one hundred.

In the Isabella Colony, the marvels of the first days gave way to desolation. The settlers were confronted by cannibalism and continual attacks from the indigenous inhabitants. Furthermore, they were struck by a new illness: syphilis, which they would bring back to Europe. In addition to all this, they lacked resources, making conditions particularly difficult. For the Native civilisation, the situation was no better; the men were exploited and the women taken from them. The only comfort to be found was the discovery of gold on Hispaniola. Christopher Columbus had therefore accomplished his mission and could return to Spain in March 1496, arriving at Cádiz on 11 June.

ANOTHER WORLD

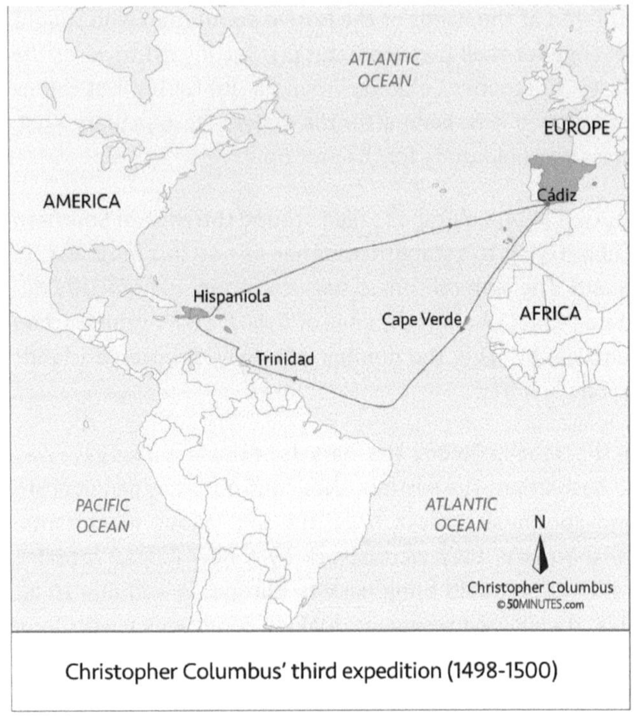

Christopher Columbus' third expedition (1498-1500)

In Spain, the euphoria of the first quest had dissipated. The reality was far-removed from the promises the admiral had made. While Spanish territory had seen several islands'-worth of expansion, these new lands did not offer the riches which had been expected; the little gold which had been found was not enough to fill the state's purse.

It was not until May 1498 that Columbus was able to depart once more with new settlers. In total, six caravels were prepared. Three of them headed straight for Hispaniola, while the other three, guided by the admiral, passed by Cape Verde in order to take an even more south-westerly route than before. This time, Columbus had his sights on reaching mainland Asia.

On 31 July, believing he had found the Indian coastline, Christopher Columbus reached South America. Little did he know that this new continent would provide all the gold they had been dreaming of. He then discovered Trinidad and the mouth of the Orinoco River. Thinking of the river's source, Columbus concluded that this land could not be India. Unable to align this new territory with the geography inherited from Antiquity, Columbus was led to the conclusion that this must be some earthly paradise: Eden.

Christopher Columbus arriving in America

Back on Hispaniola, Columbus noted that the situation had only made life in the colony worse and that the gold mine was not profitable. Rumbles of rebellion saw the admiral held responsible for this disastrous state of affairs. When civil war broke out, Columbus was forced to suspend his expedition and went on to take brutal measures, executing dissidents and redistributing the land and the Native Americans between the settlers. It is therefore clear that while Columbus was an excellent navigator, his skills as a governor left more to be desired. When the Spanish monarchs became aware of this situation, they decided to take matters into their own hands and sent a new governor to arrest Columbus and strip him of his title in August 1500. He was sent back to Spain in chains in November. Though he was soon freed in Spain, he lost his title of Viceroy and Governor of the East Indies.

IN SEARCH OF A PASSAGE TO INDIA

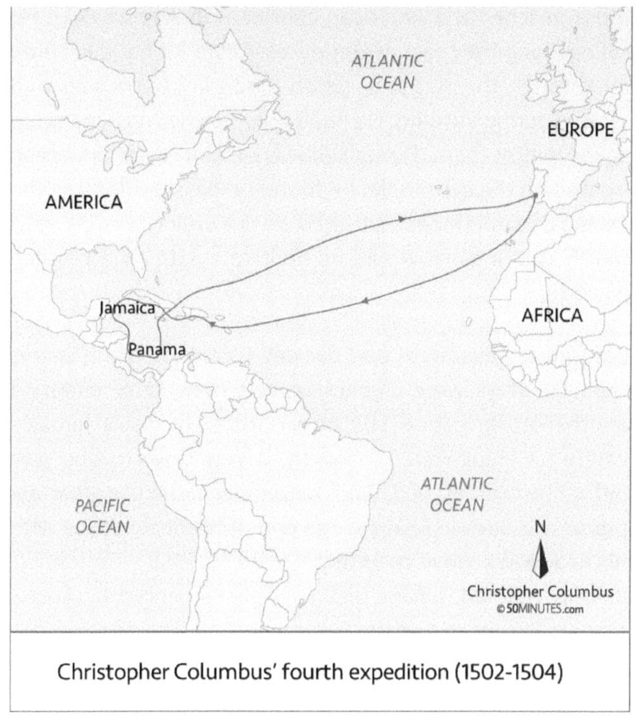

Christopher Columbus' fourth expedition (1502-1504)

Now untroubled by the trials of governance, Christopher Columbus had only one idea left in mind: return for a fourth voyage and find India. Convinced that he must locate the Strait of Malacca (between Malaysia and Indonesia) to achieve his objective, he set off on 11 May 1502 in search of this famous maritime passage.

Exiled from Hispaniola, he headed towards Cuba, taking a north-westerly then south-westerly heading and, once more, reached the American continent in August 1502. He sailed along the coast of Honduras, Costa Rica and Panama all through the summer, before enduring hurricanes and storms during autumn. He finally cast anchor on Panama to spend winter there. Though he was convinced that an ocean existed on the other side, he found no passage. In fact, the Pacific Ocean is indeed situated on the opposite coast. 400 years later, a canal would be built to create an accessible passage.

Columbus was unwell and decided to return, but it seems that the stars were aligned against him. After enduring another storm in June 1503, he was forced to stop in Jamaica where his ships were destroyed. It was close to one year before he was rescued. On 7 November 1504, the great explorer was back in Spain at the end of his final voyage with his health in a grave condition. On 20 May 1506, Columbus, died in Vallodid, having unknowingly cemented America's place in European history.

THE EXPEDITIONS' REPERCUSSIONS

GLOBAL EUROPEAN HEGEMONY

Columbus' discovery in 1492, in addition to the discovery of new routes to the East through Africa, forever changed Europe's position in the world. Though the living in the New World was a testing ordeal to the first European settlers, these lands would in time be a source of long-awaited riches. At the beginning of the 16th century, true colonial conquests were launched. These would result in the first European colonisations, from a political and economic perspective as much as with regards to religion and culture.

Stepping into the unknown, the first conquistadors, modelling themselves on Francisco Pizarro (roughly 1475-1541) and Hernan Cortez (1485-1547) seized and defeated the powerful Aztec Empire in 1521 and the Inca Empire in 1533. The gold they found made Europe rich and the commercial possibilities seemed endless. Europe, feeling constrained by its borders, threw its full weight behind this programme of expansion. Spain and Portugal were the first to establish colonial empires, but others seeking their slice of the pie were soon to follow. The British in North America, the French in Canada, the Dutch in the East: all leapt forth into the new adventure.

Unaware of the role they were playing in history, the explorers became the pioneers of globalisation, establishing a colonial system dominated by Europe which would last until the 20th century. As the new product of a long and complex process, Europe left the middle ages far behind and entered the modern era.

THE MICROBIAL SHOCK AND THE ETHNOCIDE OF THE NATIVE AMERICAN POPULATION

This European expansion was at the expense the of the Amerindian population. At first fascinated by the Spanish sailors, the indigenous inhabitants of the New World discovered the danger which the settlers represented to their civilisation all too late. While it is difficult to give an exact percentage, present day scientists agree that the Amerindian population fell dramatically when Europeans arrived.

The first victims were those of violence and war. With a hunger for profit, the settlers and conquistadors progressively enslaved the indigenous people, submitting them to forced labour and slavery. Nevertheless, the most significant cause of the rapid depopulation was a microbial shock. Having been isolated from the rest of the world for centuries, the Amerindian populations had no immunity to illnesses of European origin. As such, epidemics ensued and a common cold was enough to kill. Between one half and three quarters of the population fell victim to this microbial shock. To replace them, the Europeans began an African slave trade, during which millions of Africans were enslaved and sent to America.

The indigenous populations of America were in effect the victims of a true ethnocide. Europeans profoundly changed the political organisation of the territory and imposed their culture and religion.

Ancient Amerindian beliefs were ridiculed, which plunged the whole society into a deep depression; this population did not begin to grow again until the 18th century.

GEOGRAPHY, FOREVER CHANGED

Beyond the contrasts of some lining their pockets while others suffer tragedy, Christopher Columbus' discoveries and those of his successors marked an irreversible shift in the world's intellectual landscape. At the beginning of the 16th century, Amerigo Vespucci (Italian navigator, 1454-1512) became the first to identify the new continent for what it truly was and therefore gave it his name: America.

This significant advance perfected the geography of the time, giving rise to a whole new conception of the world. Numerous expeditions were to follow and the contours of the globe came sharply into focus; now there was a whole new world to the West between Europe and Asia.

This knowledge expansion was by no account limited to the field of geography. The Age of Discovery revolutionised navigation and climatology with the study of monsoons and trade winds. Zoologists and botanists discovered thousands of new species of life, and the appearance of new food stuffs such as potatoes and corn transformed European eating habits. The new fields of scientific research seemed endless.

Furthermore, these first exchanges between different civilisations led intellectuals to reflect on the human condition. An example of this is the Valladolid debate between Bartolomé de las Casas (Spanish theologian, 1474-1566) and Juan Ginés de Sepúlveda (Spanish theologian, 1590-1573), in which the two argued about whether the Amerindian peoples were as much human beings as the European settlers; Sepúlveda considered them to be inferior. Thus, Europeans examined their cultural conception of the human being and its place in an ever-expanding and more pluralistic world.

SUMMARY

1451
25th Aug.-31st Oct.: Christopher Columbus is born

1492
2nd Jan.: End of the Reconquista
3rd Aug.: **First expedition begins**

1493
15th Mar.: End of first expedition
25th Sept.: **Second expedition begins**

1494
7th June: Treaty of Tordeillas signed

1496
11th June: End of second expedition

1498
30th May: **Third expedition begins**

1500
25th Nov.: End of third expedition

1502
11th May: **Fourth and final expedition begins**

1504
7th Nov.: **Columbus returns to Spain forever**

1506
20th May: Christopher Columbus dies

- Christopher Columbus is born between 25 August and 31 October 1451. After several years of experience as a sailor, he makes his desire to reach the East Indies by the Atlantic Ocean known.

- After King John II refuses to finance his expedition, Columbus presents his plans at the Spanish court in front of Queen Isabella of Castile and King Ferdinand II of Aragon. At the time, they are engaged in the Reconquista and so leave Columbus' project hanging in suspense.
- Following the fall of Granada in January 1492, the Catholic monarchs agree to finance Columbus' expedition. He is named Admiral of the Ocean Sea and readies three ships for expedition: the *Pinta*, the *Niña* and the *Santa Maria*.
- Columbus sets off from Palos on 3 August 1492. After stopping on the Canary Islands, he begins his westward adventure, following the trade winds.
- The voyage is difficult for the sailors, who are confronted by unknown phenomena such as the Sea of Sargasses or unfulfilled signs of hope. They find the journey long and grow impatient. On 10 October, Columbus narrowly avoids a mutiny within the ranks.
- On 12 October 1492, the admiral finally sees land. Though unaware of it, he has just discovered a new continent: the Americas. During this first voyage, he discovers the Bahamas, Cuba and Hispaniola before returning to Spain.
- Strengthened by his success, he embarks on another quest to establish the first colony in the New World in September 1493. En route, he discovers and explores the Lesser Antilles, Southern Cuba and Jamaica. In March 1496, he returns to Spain with the hope of preparing a third voyage.
- He must wait until May 1498 before he can set off once more. Taking a more southerly route, he encounters South America for the first time. He discovers Trinidad and the mouth of the Orinoco River.

- He goes back to the colony of Spanish settlers on Hispaniola, where the situation is dire. Accused of bad governance, he is sent back to Spain in chains in 1500.
- Freed by the Spanish Crown, he begins a fourth and final journey in 1502. While his goal was to find a passage to Asia and India, he instead finds himself trapped within the coasts of Honduras, Costa Rica and Panama; he has failed in his mission.
- Tired and sick, Columbus returns to Spain, but a hurricane forces him to take refuge in Jamaica where he awaits rescue for a year. He returns to Spain in 1504 and dies two years later in Valladolid.

We want to hear from you!
Leave a comment on your online library
and share your favourite books on social media!

FIND OUT MORE

BIBLIOGRAPHY

- Almagia, R., Métraux, A., Cortesao, A. and Guyot, L. (1951) *Les conséquences de la découverte de l'Amérique par Christophe Colomb*. Paris: Palais de la découverte.
- Balard, M. (1992) *Christophe Colomb. Journal de bord 1492-1493*. Paris: Imprimerie nationale.
- Bernand, C. and Gruzinski, S. (1991) *Histoire du Nouveau Monde. De la découverte à la conquête*. Paris: Fayard.
- Favier, J. (1968) *De Marco Polo à Christophe Colomb (1250-1492)*. Paris: Larousse.
- Favier, J. (1991) *Les grandes découvertes d'Alexandre à Magellan*. Paris: Fayard.
- Heers, J. (1991) *Christophe Colomb*. Paris: Hachette.
- Todorov, T. (1982) *La conquête de l'Amérique. La question de l'autre*. Paris: Seuil.
- Various. (2006) Christophe Colomb. Magellan et le tour du monde. *Histoire universelle. L'ère des découvertes européennes*. Paris: Hachette. Volume 13.
- Various. (2006) Les découvertes géographiques des Portugais aux xve et xvie siècles. *Histoire universelle. L'ère des découvertes européennes*. Paris: Hachette. Volume 13.

ADDITIONAL SOURCES

- Mann, C. (2012) 1493: *How Europe's Discovery of the Americas Revolutionized Trade, Ecology and Life on Earth*. London: Granta Publications.
- Morison, S. E. (1975) *The European Discovery of America:*

Volume 1: The Northern Voyages, AD 500-1600. New York: Oxford University Press.
- Young, F. (2011) *Christopher Columbus and the New World of His Discovery – Complete.* London: Aeterna Press.

ICONOGRAPHIC SOURCES

- Portrait of Christopher Columbus painted in around 1835 by Antoine Maurin. Royalty-free reproduction picture.
- *Christopher Columbus before the High Council of Salamanca*, painting by Emanuel Leutze, 1841. Royalty-free reproduction picture.
- *The Surrender of Granada*, painting by Francisco Pradilla and Ortiz, 1882. Royalty-free reproduction picture.
- The caravel which would have been used during Christopher Columbus' era. Royalty-free reproduction picture.
- Painting depicting Christopher Columbus haggling over goods with the Native Americans. Royalty-free reproduction picture.
- Christoper Columbus arriving in America.
  © L. Prang & co.

FILMS AND DOCUMENTARIES

- *1492: Conquest of Paradise.* (1992) [Film]. Ridley Scott. Dir. France and Spain: Gaumont.
- *Christopher Columbus: The Discovery.* (1992) [Film]. John Glen. Dir. UK, USA and Spain: Christopher Columbus Productions.
- *Christopher Columbus: The Enigma.* (2007) [Film].

Manoel di Oliviera. Dir. Portugal: Filmes de Tejo.
* *Christopher Columbus' Maps.* (2012) [Documentary].
Paolo Santoni. Dir. France: Legardère Studios.

MUSEUMS AND COMMEMORATIVE BUILDINGS

* Columbus Lighthouse in Santo Domingo (Dominican Republic)
* Columbus Library of Seville (Spain)
* The Columbus House Museum in Valladolid (Spain)
* Replicas of the *Niña, Pinta* and *Santa Maria* in Palos (Spain)

IMPROVE YOUR GENERAL KNOWLEDGE

IN A BLINK OF AN EYE !

www.50minutes.com